Office Gender Politics Are a Battlefield

TOXIC FEMININITY

in the

WORKPLACE

Ginny Hogan

MORROW
GIFT

YES, I'M USING DATING APPS, AND 20 OTHER ANSWERS TO QUESTIONS MY COWORKERS SHOULDN'T ASK ME

1. No, I'm not sick today. I just didn't have time to put makeup on.

2. Yes, I'm tired. But I'm tired every day—you're just only noticing it today because I'm not wearing concealer.

3. No, I don't want to go to a strip club with you.

4. Yes, I watch TV shows other than *The Bachelor.* And you know what? Liking *The Bachelor* is *fine,* OK? It has nothing to do with my job performance! Maybe I just want to understand love!

5. No comment on Margot Robbie.

6. No, I would not like to beta test your new tampon-delivery service. Also, please don't ask me about it on the elevator headed to the thirtieth floor. Also, founding a new company while you're working at this company violates your contract, FYI.

7. No, I won't plan our team's offsite. I planned the last one.

8. Yes, I received the flowers you sent to my hotel room.

9. Yes, I'm still married.

10. No, I don't want to diagnose your back fungus.

11. No, I'm not thinking about having kids in the next two years.

12. Yes, I plan to keep working once I have kids.

13. No, I don't think it's impossible to be a good mother and have a successful career.

14. Yes, I am on birth control.

15. Yes, I bought this at Victoria's Secret.

16. No, I don't think *Infinite Jest* is the most brilliant book ever written. It was good, but a little long.

17. No, I don't want to hear your opinion.

18. No, thank you.

19. No.

20. Ew, no.

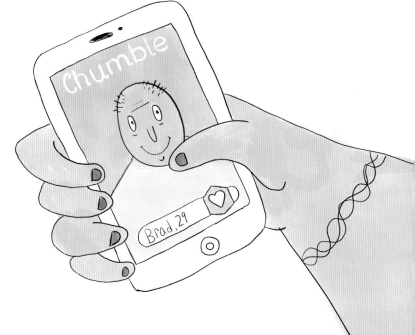

PERKS TECH START-UPS ADDED TO RECRUIT MORE WOMEN

- Manicure station on first Fridays.

- A discounted stylist.

- Free birth control.

- Access to a small number of cute single men.

- Access to a large number of single men.

- Egg-freezing. You can always have kids later!

- Free dry cleaning.

- Complementary therapist to ask if you *really* think right now is a good time to have children. And if you say yes, she (it'll be a woman, obviously) will ask again, but this time more slowly.

- A salad bar exactly once a month.

- Free in-house adoption agency. Why not? We can put those kids to work—there's a lot of data that can't be cleaned programmatically.

Perks Tech Start-ups Forgot to Add to Recruit More Women

- Parental leave.

- Equal pay.

AN UNCONSCIOUS BIAS TRAINING TO TEACH MEN TO NOT TOUCH THEIR FEMALE COWORKERS

Hi, thanks for coming to my training today. Here, we're going to teach you all about unconscious biases, specifically those that cause you to touch your female coworkers.

Everyone has unconscious biases. They're what make us associate engineering words like *build* and *bridge* with men and liberal-arts words like *book* and *emotions* with women. We don't have much control over which unconscious biases we have—they were given to us by society, and, according to my therapist and mother, we're pretty much stuck with them. But what we do have control over is how we respond to them. We need to be made aware of our unconscious biases so we can stop them from affecting our lives.

For many of you, when you see a woman, you probably have the urge to touch her. This is, in fact, an unconscious bias. You're biased to believe that touching a woman will make your and her lives better, but I'm here to tell you today—it will not. In fact, you will probably get in trouble with the HR department, fired, and then blacklisted from the tech industry. Probably. I don't make the rules. Bad things will happen to her too, but who's paying attention?

Of course, if there's anything I want this training to impart on you, men, it's that it's not *your fault* that you want to touch women. It's *society's fault*. So if you've accidentally grabbed your boss's ass, don't beat yourself up over it! But do be aware of the unconscious biases you have, and do your best to work around them. Even if you fail, I can probably get you off the hook if you at least try. Next up in your schedule is my other training, an Unconscious Bias Training to Teach Men to Treat Their Female Coworkers Like People.

THE SEXISM CONSPIRACY

Matt sat down at his desk, disgruntled. He'd been called out in a meeting for speaking over a woman. But you know what—she wasn't speaking *that* loudly, so how could it be his fault? Besides, he knew for a fact that he was paid as much as the woman, so his opinion was just as valid—she was only, like, a few years more experienced, a decade tops. Sometimes, and he felt guilty for thinking this, but sometimes, only sometimes, he really thought maybe women just *made sexism up*.

Susan swiveled around in her chair, watching Matt's brain waves through her monitor. "Goddamnit," she said, "they're onto us."

"What?!" Lizzie gasped.

"The men are starting to figure us out. They know what we're doing."

"You don't mean . . ."

"I do. They've uncovered The Sexism Conspiracy."

Lizzie was dismayed. "How can this be?!!"

"I thought that banning the Men's Rights subreddits would be enough, but it's not. Their accurate theories have made their way into the mainstream. Men are beginning to realize that there's actually no disadvantage to being a woman—that sexism is a hoax invented by women to get Hollywood to produce more rom-coms."

Lizzie started tearing up. "I really thought we'd covered our tracks well. I thought giving women less money and fewer rights, sticking them with nearly all the housework, the 2016 presidential election, painful IUD insertions—I thought that would be enough! Do you think they know everything? Do they know about the math—"

"Looks like it. Soon everyone will know that men have actually always believed women can do math, and that women just invented the stereotype so that all female heroines in rom-coms have a consistent quirk."

"What about the sound of our voices?"

"Men are starting to figure out that they're biologically predisposed to think a person is *more* intelligent the higher the pitch. In fact, before long, we should expect children to be running companies, much like Mark Zuckerberg," Susan told her.

"This comes at a dire time," she continued. "We haven't had a good romantic comedy since *The Big Sick*. Netflix is producing some content, but is any of it good?"

Lizzie shook her head no. She hadn't watched, but she'd heard it was bad. I mean, it just *looked* bad.

"It's shocking, isn't it?" Susan continued, "After all we've taken away from women just to perpetuate the false idea that sexism exists, men *still* realized we were making it up. They know there's nothing hard about being a woman. They've discovered that systemic biases are actually just in *women's heads*. How'd they figure it out!?"

"Men might be smarter than we've given them credit for. Maybe they really did earn all those Nobel Prizes we rigged for them. Maybe we were right to forcefully keep women out of technical academic fields! What happens now?" Lizzie asked.

Susan took a deep breath. "It's not going to be good. Once men no longer feel guilty about sexism, they'll realize there's really no reason to be nice to women. They'll stop developing products specifically for us—in particular, pink razors and romantic comedies."

Lizzie was in tears. Her life's work had been to promote The Sexism Conspiracy. Sure, she'd gotten women the right to vote back in the 1920s, but she'd known that wasn't meant to be her magnum opus. Rom-coms made their debut back then. Once *It Happened One Night* came out, she recognized her true mission: she had to get society to believe women still had a specific damsel-in-distress place in the world so that Hollywood producers would make movies about it. It was the only thing keeping her going at age 203! And now it was slipping away, one meet-cute at a time.

"Maybe we have some time. Kate Hudson's career isn't over yet—maybe we could squeeze a few more hits out of her," Susan replied calmly.

"I don't know—have you seen her haircut?" Lizzie wailed.

"Hair grows back. At least, for women."

"But what do we do about the men who are catching on?!" Lizzie sobbed.

"Well, this isn't a long-term solution, but we can extinguish them on an as-needed basis," Susan said. "Take comfort—*13 Going on 30* will be available on demand until the end of time."

"Extinguish them?"

"Yes. Don't you know—we actually control their heart functionality. We mostly use it to make their hearts beat faster when an attractive actress is on screen so they'll keep watching Katherine Heigl movies, but it has other uses." Susan pressed the pink button.

At his desk, Matt suddenly began to clutch his chest. *Was this just terrible indigestion? Or the three Rockstars he had with lunch? He was only twenty-seven!* He crumpled to the floor.

TRANSCRIPT OF A MEETING WHERE NO WOMEN GET INTERRUPTED

Janet: Hey everyone, thanks for coming to the meeting today. We'd like to discuss our pitch for investors next week. Did everyone (pauses) did everyone get the PowerPoint?

Everyone nods.

Boris: Thanks for sending it, Janet.

Janet: What are our thoughts?

Kara raises her hand.

Janet: Yes, Kara.

Kara: I think on page two we need to reiterate our company goal.

Fred: That's a great idea. I have an idea of how to do it, but I'd love to hear your suggestions first.

Kara: Let's say "We seek to provide an automated solution to your servicing needs."

Fred: That's even better than the idea I had!

Arnold: We should give Kara credit for her idea because it's hers. All of it. Even the part I had also thought of—she still said it, and I didn't.

Liz: That's great. I have another idea. (pauses) Would you like to hear it?

Everyone nods 'yes' emphatically, but not too emphatically, an appropriate amount of excitement for a workplace meeting.

Liz: I think we should delete slide eight because it's redundant with slide sixteen.

Fred: You're absolutely right.

Boris: We should definitely remove slide eight.

Arnold: I was also going to suggest removing slide eight.

Everyone gives him a dirty look.

Arnold: But it was definitely Liz's idea! Let's give her the credit. As we already have.

Janet: Does anyone else have any notes?

Everyone nods no.

Janet: Wow, that was wildly short and efficient. You can take the extra twenty minutes as part of your lunch break. And you'll all be getting a bonus for your efficiency gains!

Everyone cheers, even Arnold.

QUIZ: AS A WOMAN, ARE YOU TOO AGGRESSIVE, OR ARE YOU POLITELY STATING YOUR OPINION?

Your boss asks you if you want to work over the weekend on a project that doesn't need to be completed for three months. You say:

A. I've been working overtime for the last two months–do you think there's someone else on the team who could help me?

B. I'm sorry, my sister's getting married in Napa this weekend. I can work late next week to get it done.

Your teammate asks what you think of his PowerPoint. You notice a typo on slide two. You say:

A. Thank you so much for sending me this PowerPoint! I really appreciate it. I fixed one typo on page two.

B. Hey, on slide two, you wrote "thb" when you meant "the." Other than that, great deck!

You're at a work dinner. You order a chicken dish with no peppers, but the waiter tells you the peppers are baked in. You say:

> **A.** Ah, OK, I'll eat around them.

> **B.** No problem! I'm allergic to peppers though, so I'll get the salmon.

Your CEO credits your male coworker for a project you completed. You say:

> **A.** I'm just glad someone was able to get it done.

> **B.** Barry did great work on this, but actually, we collaborated. I look forward to working with him more in the future!

Your coworker gets an ugly haircut. You say:

> **A.** Nice haircut.

> **B.** Nothing.

Mostly A's: You're WAY too aggressive!! Didn't your mother teach you any manners?

Mostly B's: CALM DOWN!! You are being *so* insanely aggressive—you should be ashamed of yourself!

A mix of A's and B's: Take a Xanax already! This is no place for your aggression!

IF YOU GIVE A MAN A COMPLIMENT ON HIS MEDIOCRE JOB PERFORMANCE

He's going to ask for a raise.

When you give him the raise, he'll probably ask for a title change as well.

When he's finished, he'll assume he deserves another compliment for successfully navigating the system.

Then he'll want to look in the mirror and confirm that his new job comes with its own bathroom.

When he looks in the mirror, he'll notice his beard needs a trim, so he'll probably take the rest of the day off to shave it.

When he's finished with his day off, he'll want a vacation to cement his new position.

When he takes a vacation, he might realize he needs to buy a summer home in Nantucket.

To afford his summer home in Nantucket, he'll need another raise, which he'll get, because he's a man.

When he gets his second raise, his female coworkers may start gossiping about the fact that he's now getting paid twice what they do even though he's less competent.

Once his female coworkers start gossiping, they'll also ask for raises, but they'll be unlikely to receive them because they're women, and also because this man is their new boss.

After the women who now work for him (even though they're significantly more qualified) start asking for raises, he's going to have to start blocking out his entire Google Calendar to avoid meetings.

If he blocks off his Google Calendar, the executives at the company are going to think he's extremely important, and they're going to give him another raise.

When he's done, he'll probably need a fine scotch! And a nap!

2019 BECHDEL TEST, UPDATED FOR WOMEN AT WORK

Hi there, ladies! Do you work at a mostly male company? Are you wondering if your conversations with your female coworkers pass the classic Bechdel test? We've updated the test for 2019 to answer that question for you.

1. Does your conversation with a female coworker last more than ten minutes before one of you reveals that you've been sexually harassed?

2. Does your team meeting include any woman speaking for more than thirty seconds without being interrupted?

3. Do you feel like your male coworkers listen to you literally ever?

4. You just started a new job. Can you go one week without your female coworkers telling you which man is the biggest perpetrator of workplace sexual harassment? When they tell you, are you surprised, or was it already obvious? Was it Fred?

5. Do you have any problems in your life that you could attribute to something other than the patriarchy? What about acid reflux? Do you have acid reflux? That might be a problem unrelated to the patriarchy. You know what, though—if you have acid reflux due to increased consumption of wine, that could also be the patriarchy.

6. Are you OK?

If you answered Yes to any of the above questions, or thought about answering Yes to any of them, congratulations! You passed the Bechdel test. Your job seems fine—stop complaining about it.

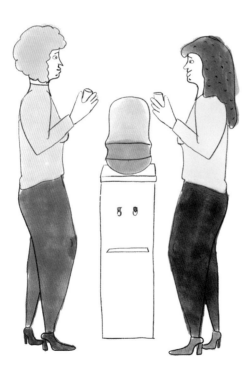

NEGOTIATIONS

"Look, it's never going to feel like the right time," Donna warned her. "But if you don't do it now, you'll be in the same position forever."

Zoe knew she was right. She'd been at the company for eight years and hadn't gotten so much as a title change. She worked day in and day out, often coming in on weekends to keep the ship running smoothly. She'd been a perfect executive assistant, and her boss, Matt, had assured her the job would lead to more. He promised she could move up in another department—maybe recruiting, maybe design. She didn't have a clear idea of what she wanted to do, but she knew it was time for a change.

"OK, I'll schedule the meeting," Zoe told Donna.

"Great. Just remember—it's all about asking for what you want and knowing your worth."

"But what is my worth? I've had the same salary for eight years!"

Donna put her hand up against Zoe's heart. "It's your intrinsic worth. The one we all have as individuals. Seventy grand a year, at least."

"And if he says no?"

"You have to be prepared to give him an ultimatum. You need to do it. For *all* women."

Zoe sighed. The thought of finding a new job was overwhelming, but Donna was right, again—if she didn't threaten Matt, he might never be incentivized to promote her.

The next day, Zoe put a meeting for the two of them on his calendar. Matt didn't know what it was about. In fact, he was so clueless about Zoe's dissatisfaction that he didn't even have a guess. Zoe knocked on his door.

"Come in."

Zoe took a seat. "Hey Matt, there's something I've been meaning to talk to you about."

"Shoot."

"OK, well, I've been your assistant for eight years. I think I've done a really great job—I have here a list of all my accomplishments, by year. You said you thought after a few years I could get a promotion, and I'm wondering if that's something you still see happening."

Matt sighed. "Zoe, you know I value you more than my own stupid wife, but I can't promote you right now. We're so tight on cash, and we just hired Deborah. I hope you understand."

Zoe looked at him sadly. "I do, but you know, I'm not just going to stay your assistant forever. You know what this means, right? You know what I have to do?"

Matt cringed. He knew what was coming—he'd seen it happen to bosses before. He hated the thought of having to give his own life, but what other options were there? The company was simply out of cash. He got down on his knees and stuck his head out. Zoe took a chain saw out of her laptop bag and covered his head with a size 7 Jiffy bag.

On the way out, Zoe made eye contact with Donna. Donna saw the chain saw and gave her a big thumbs-up. Zoe wiped her brow. It was hard, but she was proud that she'd stood up for herself. And women everywhere.

IF WOMEN ASSESSED MALE CANDIDATES
THE WAY MEN ASSESS WOMEN

Lisa: I thought he was very qualified. He answered my questions well, and his code was impeccable. I had just one slight concern—he was wearing an *awful* lot of hair gel. Are we sure he has a professional-enough look for this company?

Teresa: I'm glad you brought that up. I was also put off by his physical appearance. In fact, I couldn't really concentrate on what he was saying because of the hair gel. And I should add that *my* inability to focus because of *his* appearance is entirely *his* problem, not mine. I shouldn't have to do extra work to listen to his answers when I can *literally* smell the gel from across the room.

Annie: I had mixed feelings. On the one hand, he has the perfect work experience, and he scored well on my technical assessment. On the other hand, he used the word "bro" to describe his roommate. I'm just not really comfortable with someone who uses speech patterns like that—it made him look stupid, and I think he should stop.

Maureen: While he impressed me during the interview, he also told me over lunch that he doesn't like to watch *Sex and the City,* so I just can't see him fitting into the culture.

Tonya: Did you see his wedding ring? *Somebody* is probably going to have kids in a few years. I just don't want to hire him and then risk having him take three days of paternity leave!

Janet: He was just a little too good-looking to work here. It would be distracting.

A REVIEW OF *LEAN OUT:* A SELF-HELP BOOK TEACHING MEN TO STOP TALKING FOR ONCE

Lean Out is a powerful self-help book for men in the workplace. Not everyone knows this, but many men have to work to support themselves. Sometimes, they unwittingly find themselves in offices that include women. *Lean Out* gives men the skills they need to survive in a workplace with women, namely the skills to close their damn mouths and shut the hell up for once.

Lean Out covers how men should behave in business meetings. In order for men to exist peacefully in the workplace, the author recommends that they stop talking sometimes. This isn't to say men should *never* speak, it's just a suggestion that a man who is at work eight hours a day should spend no more than five of those hours with his mouth running. The other three hours can be spent doing a variety of tasks such as getting coffee, checking email, or napping. In special circumstances, men can even consider filling their non-talking hours with the responsibilities of their jobs. I know this sounds like a big adjustment for men who are used to talking 100 percent of the time, but rest assured, with a few simple changes, you, too, can learn to not speak at all waking moments.

The author of *Lean Out* gives some practical tips for how men can shut up on occasion. Her main proposal is the "Four-Second Rule." It's similar to the three-second rule but without dirty food. The Four-Second Rule states that when your female coworker starts speaking, you should listen to what she says for at least four seconds. Then, after four seconds, if you're absolutely sure what you have to say is more interesting or relevant, you are free to speak over her. As with a YouTube ad model, economists estimate this could save $60 billion a year.

The main problem with *Lean Out* is that it contains a lot of words written by a woman. The target audience is men who don't like to read or hear things said by a woman, so it's hard to imagine this book will do well financially.

The author accounts for this on the cover, in which she attributes the book to "YOU AND ONLY YOU, YOU SMART MAN YOU." Much like J. K. Rowling, she knows that men won't read a book written by women, but unlike J. K. Rowling, her book is for adult men and not little boys. Hopefully, convincing men that they actually wrote the book will help draw more male readers.

Lean Out can be purchased for $0.00 on Amazon and at your local bookstore. The author has chosen to make it free as a public service to literally everyone.

"GIRLS DIDN'T LIKE ME IN COLLEGE" AND NINE OTHER REASONS YOUR COWORKER THINKS IT'S FINE TO NOT RESPECT WOMEN

1. My mom was mean to me once.

2. The one girl in my computer science class in college wouldn't hook up with me.

3. The HR lady at my last job had a back tattoo.

4. I got dumped on my birthday.

5. Ann Coulter—need I say more?

6. #notallmen

7. A bitch cut me off today in traffic. I actually couldn't tell if it was a woman, but I assume so because I was mad after it happened.

8. It's impossible for white men to get jobs anymore. I mean, I got one, and so did 80 percent of the office, but it's getting harder, o-kay?

9. It's not fair that only women get to show their feelings *sniffle*.

SO YOUR BOSS ASKED YOU TO PICK UP HIS DRY CLEANING

It's your second week as a software engineer, and something strange has happened: your boss just asked you to pick up his dry cleaning. *Why*, you ask? Because his assistant is out on vacation. Picking up his dry cleaning is definitely NOT your job, so here are some helpful tips to handle this situation.

· Tell him you're busy with work. Remind him of all the programming projects you're working on *as his employee*.

· Ask him if any of your male colleagues are free to handle this. Perhaps one who works under you, like an intern?

· Ponder what he needs to get dry cleaned, considering he wears jeans (presumably dirty) and a T-shirt to work every day.

· Suggest one of the many on-demand apps through which he might hire someone to complete tasks for him. For example, he could use the services of TaskRabbit, the app that you both work for.

· Pretend not to hear him when he makes this absurd request.

· Feign ignorance and claim you don't speak English.

· Search for a new job.

· Tell him to PICK UP HIS OWN DAMN DRY CLEANING.

IF TECH PRODUCTS WERE REMADE BY WOMEN

Do you ever wonder how your favorite tech products would change if they had been created by women?

- **Instagram:** If womInstagram were created by women, you wouldn't be able to slide into anyone's DM. You'd have to knock loudly at their door and wait a while for them to answer.
- **Uber:** In the new and improved Ub-her, passengers would get a one-star review for trying to hit on their poolmates.
- **Venmo:** Using womEnmo, you wouldn't see other people's transactions so you wouldn't know who the new girl going to Dave Matthews with your ex is.
- **Tinder:** A female-designed Tind-for-her wouldn't let men send the first message—oh, wait, that already exists, it's called Bumble, and it's awesome!
- **Podcasts:** When women make a pod-fast, the default speed is 1.5x. Men are slow.
- **Alexa:** Alex would be voiced by a man. We'd yell our orders at him.
- **Facebook:** Macebook would stop asking us to constantly tell our whole social network our location and would spray people who visit our profiles too frequently.

- **Hulu:** The female-designed Lucy-Liu would only show Lucy Liu movies because she's amazing!
- **Twitter:** Wit-her would increase the character limit only for those with something *interesting* and *useful* and *not hateful* to say.
- **Reddit:** Imagine a world where reddit was created by women and all the users were women. Read-it! So literary! There would be no hate speech!
- **Weather.com:** This would stay the same because this site is already perfect.

HONEST CAPTIONS FOR PHOTOS ON YOUR COMPANY'S DIVERSITY PAGE

Here, we see two female engineers working together. These two women aren't on the same team and have never shared a project, but Tina is giving Elizabeth advice on Airbnb houses in L.A.

Notice that the finance team in this photo appears to be only half men! Not pictured: Bennett, Todd, Dan, Paul, Dennis, and Fred.

SKIPE

This is bring-your-child-to-work day–it is definitely NOT the CEO asking his assistant to babysit for him.

You'll notice this group of employees is particularly diverse! That's because we borrowed them from the company downstairs.

QUIZ: ARE YOU A TRUE FEMINIST, A MALE FEMINIST, A FEMINIST JUST TO GET LAID, OR A LOAF OF BREAD?

Men, this is the time to ask yourself—what kind of feminist are you? Not all feminists are equally good (although all men are very, very good), so here, we find out just which type you are.

Your male colleague speaks over a female colleague at work. Do you:

    A. Cut him off and say you'd like to hear what *she* had to say.

    B. Cut him off and point out how *you'd* never interrupt a woman.

    C. Cut him off, tell him he interrupted her, and then very conspicuously shoot her a wink.

    D. Sit there like an inanimate mound of flour and yeast.

You see a man talking to a woman on the train. She has her headphones in and tries to ignore him. Do you:

A. Give her your seat so she can get away from him.

B. Walk up to him and shove him, thereby drawing attention to what a feminist icon you are. You later post a five-paragraph essay about it on Facebook.

C. Interrupt their conversation to talk to her. When she thanks you and turns away, keep talking at her even though she has her headphones in. Give her a wink.

D. Taste better with garlic and butter.

In your district, a female Democrat in favor of universal healthcare is running against a male incumbent Republican in favor of Trump. Do you:

A. Vote for her.

B. Vote for her and shed judgment on everyone who didn't.

C. Vote for him but don't tell anyone. Wink twice to yourself in the voting booth.

D. Bemoan the fact that the Fifteenth Amendment extends not to carbs.

The women at your company inform you that the men are being paid more. Do you:

A. Tell them you'll support them if they want to bring this up to HR.

B. Ask if they've considered that maybe it's because they exercised their *constitutional right* to take lower-paying jobs.

C. Tell them you'll buy them a drink to even things out. Then wink.

D. Grow mold if left out for too long.

You notice friends of yours are giving their eight-year-old son blocks and their six-year-old daughter dolls. Do you:

A. Ask them if their daughter might like blocks for her birthday.

B. Loudly comment on this gendered behavior at a dinner party.

C. Loudly comment on this gendered behavior at a dinner party and tell the single woman sitting next to you what a *progressive* father you'd be. Wink some more.

D. Jump into the toaster in a suicide attempt but come out even more delicious than before.

You encounter a woman crying on a park bench. Do you:

A. LEAVE HER ALONE.
People should be allowed to cry in peace.

B. Sit down next to her and let her know everything's going to be fine–*you're* there.

C. Put your arm around her and promise you're better than that guy she's crying over. Wink eight more times.

D. Offer her yourself with melted cheese on top and be the first man to ever make a crying woman actually feel better.

HOW TO MAKE YOURSELF PHYSICALLY RESEMBLE MARK ZUCKERBERG TO GET MORE VENTURE CAPITAL FUNDING

"I can be tricked by anyone who looks like Mark Zuckerberg."
—Paul Graham

You want funding for your start-up? It's easy! All you have to do is coif yourself to resemble Mark Zuckerberg. Here are some Zucker-tips:

· **Dress casually:** Showing up in a gray T-shirt and jeans demonstrates that you don't care about the way you present yourself, and that's cool. Don't wear a skirt. Mark Zuckerberg would never wear a skirt.
· **Look disinterested:** If there's one thing Mark Zuckerberg knows how to do, it's look bored. And be rich. But while looking bored. Stay on your phone the whole time—don't make any eye contact with the VCs in the room.
· **Be twenty years old:** Botox botox botox. Maybe a facelift. Get those tits perky, if you have them. There's a reason it's called "Silicone" valley.
· **Be a man:** While seeming to contradict the last point about perky tits, it's actually very easy to pretend to be a man. Have you ever seen *Shakespeare in Love*?
· **Be white:** This one is pretty straightforward.

PUT SOME TIME ON YOUR CALENDAR

JUNEUARY

SON	MUN	TOOS	WEN	TRUS	FRY	SAT
	1 TIME	2	3	4	5 TIME	6
7 TIME	8	9 TIME	10	11 TIME	12	13
14 TIME	15	16 TIME	17 TIME	18 TIME	19 TIME	20
21	22	23	24 TIME	25	26	27 TIME
28 TIME	29	30 TIME	31			

Susy sits at her desk. It's already 10 a.m. She'd gotten to work at seven, but she is just now getting around to her project. Her calendar is so busy with meetings that the mornings seem like the only time to get things done. Unfortunately, this morning she is bogged down by multiple calls with East Coast clients. Just then, Tim pokes his head from behind her desk.

"Hey, Susy, can I put some time on your calendar later to discuss the mortgage product?" he asks. "It'll just be a quick meeting, one hour tops."

Susy sighs, and before she has agreed, Tim sends her a Google Calendar invite. She looks at her calendar for the day: back-to-back meetings until 7 p.m. Tim has just taken over her lunch break.

Will approaches. "Hey, I added some time to your calendar to go over the edits on Matt's presentation," he tells her.

"But I don't have any more time on my calendar," Susy replies, confident that she simply couldn't fit it in.

"No," Will says, "I *added time* to your calendar."

Susy looks at her calendar again. Did it—look longer? She squints. Were there two slots for 2:00 p.m. Right there: 2:00 p.m., call Frank; 2:00 p.m., Will Meeting Matt Edits.

"How will I do both?" She asks.

"I put some time on your calendar. I got you an extra 2:00 p.m.," Will tells her and walks off.

Susy is confused. She doesn't know what will happen when 2:00 p.m. rolls around. At 1:59, Frank calls. She considers telling him to keep it brief because she has another meeting, but he launches into a long pitch for how to overhaul their retail strategy. He wants Susy to take it to the CEO. She takes notes, anxiously looking at her email, wondering if Will is about to send her an angry message for missing their meeting.

At 2:30 on the dot, Frank hangs up. Susy goes back to her computer again, but something strange happens—the clock says 2:00 p.m. No—that couldn't be right. She does what any sane woman would do and googles what time it is. 2:00 p.m. 5:00:00 p.m. on the East Coast. She asks her cubicle mate. 2:00 p.m., he says. She tries to triangulate time from the sun's location, but she simply isn't outdoorsy enough! Will approaches her desk.

"You ready?" He asks, "I booked room 5b."

"But—I don't understand—I just got off a thirty-minute call that started at two—how is it . . ."

"I told you I'd put time on your calendar," Will says with a wink.

The next day, Susy's requests for time on her calendar double. It seems like everyone at the company wants a meeting with her. And her schedule just expands to fill time. It's like magic! She still never has any time to work on her own projects, but she is able to help literally everyone else at the company.

It continues for weeks. Susy has taken on everyone else's job responsibilities. The company is more profitable than it's been in years. Everyone who needs a favor from Susy gets one—all they have to do is add some time to the magic calendar. After a few months, Susy knocks on the CEO's door.

"I'm quitting," she says.

"WHAT?!! WHY!?" he asks in shock.

"I'm on the verge of a nervous breakdown. I've been working thirty-two-hour days for over a month," Susy says, collapsing from stress on the spot.

The CEO stares at her limp body on the floor, shaking his head. "Too bad she didn't put some time on her calendar to rest."

LETTERS FROM THE CEO: UNFORTUNATELY, I'M TOO BUSY CURING DEATH TO FOCUS ON HIRING MORE WOMEN

Hi, everyone. Thanks for coming to the all-hands. I know there have been some questions recently about the representation of women at our wonderful tech company. I just want to reassure all of you—I hear you. I agree that it would be better if more than 15 percent of our employees were women. Maybe we should hire a second female engineer. Oh, what's that? Katie quit? Ah, well. Sadly, though, I just haven't had time in the last year to focus at all on diversity because I'm *very* busy with curing death.

Yes, I know what you're thinking—death can't be cured. But you know what? Before Google came along, they said we'd never have infinite knowledge. And now we do. I literally know everything. Before Facebook was invented, all the haters said, "Mark, we'll never all be friends." And now we are. Every single person in the world is friends with each other. Before Snapchat,

we thought our poop photos would live forever and our bodies would die. Anyway, the point I'm trying to get across is: No one thought we'd cure death until we sat down and did it. Which we will do in the future, which will then be infinite.

How am I going to cure death? Well, first, I'll bring in some male scientists. Oh, sorry, I'll bring in some scientists, all of whom will probably be male, statistically speaking. And then I'll put them to work developing a method to ward off death. Because death is a choice. Every morning when we wake up, we can choose to live or die. So to cure death, I'm simply going to ask all of you to live. Each day, wake up next to your girlfriend or wife—oh, sorry, some of you might have boyfriends or husbands, I'd hate for anyone to think I was homophobic—anyway, wake up next to your partner—yes, I know a lot of you are understandably single, but just go with it—wake up next to your partner or empty bed, and say, "Today, I choose to live." And you do that every day, and then, viola, death is cured!

Why am I choosing to focus on death? Well, here's the thing. Diversity is important to many, but it doesn't affect *me*. In fact, it doesn't affect a lot of the people in this room right now, which I think is what someone was getting at—never mind, OK. I just know that I'll be more devoted to a project if I'm doing it from a place of passion and self-absorption. So I analyzed all problems facing me at this moment in time, and I realized I have two problems: traffic on the 101 and I'm going to die. There's literally nothing that can be done to ward off traffic, so I am focusing my energy on curing death.

Any other questions for me? OK, yes, I know. The last female engineer, Katie, quit because her manager grabbed her ass. How many times are you going to keep reminding me of that?! I feel that your constant email reminders are a violation of my personal space. Yes, we need to turn our attention to making sure women feel safe and respected in this environment. We should probably implement a human resources manual—I mean, we are seventy thousand employees now. The time is ripe. And maybe we should fire Grab-Ass-Tad. But I don't have time to do any of that right now because I'm meeting with futurists to plan the next seven hundred years of my life.

The great news, though, is that after I've cured death, I'll be alive forever, so I'll have all of eternity to bring in more female engineers. If we grow our engineering team at the rate of one new female engineer per decade, we'll have equal representation in the year 2659, which we will all live to see, thanks to me. And when women reap the benefits of my hard work, they'll have an infinite lifetime of men talking over them in meetings to look forward to! It's like *Groundhog Day,* except starring a woman, so it won't win any Oscars.

After I cure death, I want to assure you all that I will turn my focus entirely toward improving diversity at this large tech company. Right after I build a flying car and bring Marilyn Monroe back to life AS AN EXPERIMENT and not at all because I'd LIKE TO HAVE SEX WITH HER. Thank you for your time. Free beer in the back.

MY MALE COWORKERS TEACH ME HOW WOMEN USE THE INTERNET

At my current tech start-up, I'm learning all sorts of things from my male co-workers about female internet behavior. This precious knowledge is how all-male start-ups are building wonderful products for their female counterparts.

Notes on Advertising:

- Women like when Amazon learns that they're women and advertises them exclusively makeup products.
- Women get their news from only PopSugar and Twitter—don't try to advertise to them on nytimes.com.
- Women want their Chrome homepage to default to victoriassecret.com. If they change it, assume they made a mistake, and automatically change it back.
- Women buy too much useless stuff. Advertise them "stuff."

Notes on Social Media:

- Check a woman's Facebook search history if you want to know exactly whom she's interested in boning. There's no way she'd ever just search for her friends. If a woman searches you on Facebook, she wants to have sex with you.

- If a woman sees a friend change her Facebook profile picture and does NOT like it, it means she hates her. They've probably slept with the same guy. This is the only reason women get into fights.
- If a woman is older than thirty, do NOT remind her that it's her birthday on Facebook. All women are terrified of aging, and they all know that getting a year older is the worst thing that's ever happened to a woman older than twenty-four.
- Every woman will stop posting selfies on Instagram three days out of the month because her period makes her feel fat and unattractive.
- Women who use reddit are asking for it.

Notes on Body Image:

- Women only watch cat videos and eyeliner tutorials on YouTube. Don't bother recommending them any other type of content. If you advertise them a Pilates video, you'll make them feel bad about themselves.
- Women would never buy clothing online because they're all lying to themselves about their dress sizes.
- Women LOVE food-delivery apps because they feel ashamed about eating or purchasing food in public.

Notes on Dating:

- It's impossible to be a straight man on dating apps because women only swipe right on men who are taller than them and make a lot of money. And there are literally no straight men who are taller than a woman and make money.

- Everyone's Venmo history needs to be public because women look at what their ex-boyfriends are up to every day. This is information they need to have, or else they, like, don't function.
- Women do not think clearly when they're menstruating, so do NOT let them book a flight during their time of the month. They will most likely book a flight they can't afford to visit an ex-boyfriend who doesn't love them anymore and possibly never did.

Notes on Fear-Based Browsing:

- Women mostly use the internet to check their horoscopes.
- Women believe the dark web is just websites with a black background, so they avoid these sites. This includes Netflix, of course, so just know that every woman who seems to have a Netflix account actually only keeps it around for her ex-boyfriends to use and remember her by.
- Women don't use the internet after 11:00 p.m. because they're so scared of the dark.
- Women are scared to bank online because they worry they might get abducted by aliens. Ignore aforementioned notes about Venmo, since we all know Venmo dollars aren't real dollars.
- Women fear websites that begin with the letter *T*—it's an old wives' tale—do NOT bring it up. They think websites like twitter.com can lead to early death or even acne.
- Women are also scared of Craigslist because, like, I don't know? It's irrational. What harm could possibly come to a woman on Craigslist? It's like how some women are scared of "walking in parks" at "night." It's just like a strange quirk that we have to accept if we want to truly be allies.

AS THE FATHER OF A DAUGHTER, IT UPSETS ME THAT WOMEN DON'T GET PAID AS MUCH, BECAUSE WHO WILL SUPPORT ME IN MY OLD AGE?

I worked for fifteen years before I had my daughter. I had never thought highly of the women I worked with—why were they always complaining about their salaries? It seemed like all of them made enough money to buy clothes, what more could they need? My wife—she didn't work. I preferred it that way. But then, as I looked into the eyes of my newborn baby girl, I realized something—women *do* deserve to be paid as much as men. Because who else is going to support me when I retire?

My little girl—she's really something. She's precocious and smart, and I know she's going to be successful someday. It's so critical that we fight for equal pay, and I know my daughter will make a lot of money. At least, I really hope she's going to make a lot of money because I took out two mortgages on this house and I was thinking maybe she'd be able to pay them off for me when she's twenty-five.

The other day, my darling five-year-old girl built a sandcastle so beautiful I knew she was going to be an architect. And it's important to me that we make sure architecture as a field lets more women in and pays them equally! I posted a Facebook status about that because I'm a feminist and I am doing my part! Also, her sandcastle reminded me that I've always wanted a beach house on Martha's Vineyard, and hopefully she'll buy me one. Let's keep up the good fight and make sure women make as much money as men. And for my daughter, ideally I'd like her to earn ten times the median salary, and I will make this known to her repeatedly for the rest of her childhood.

HOW TO SIT SO YOUR MALE COLLEAGUE WON'T THINK YOU WANT TO HAVE SEX WITH HIM

So you're about to have a business meeting with a man. The biggest challenge of meetings is figuring out where to sit so that you don't indicate a sexual desire for your male colleague. It's difficult, because men are known for picking up signals of sexual interest from business coffees and all other places. Here, we offer a helpful guide of where you can place your bum for any seating arrangement.

Square Table with Four Chairs

If your partner sits down before you, you need to sit exactly opposite to him, but you must pull your chair to one side of the opposite edge so that you're not straining to hear him. Do NOT sit at one of the edges adjacent to him—that's too close for comfort, and he will think you're coming on to him.

Square Table with Two Chairs

If there are only two chairs and they are on adjacent sides, you must pick a chair and then slowly scooch away from your male colleague during the entirety of the meeting. Focus all your energy on scooching away and not on what he is saying. It probably wasn't that relevant anyway.

Round Table with Three Chairs

The circle is an inherently sexual shape (tits? beach balls? men's balls? I've made my point), so you need to be extra careful about where you sit. Anywhere you sit around a round table will lead your partner to conclude you want sex with him, so it's best to just say you're going to the bathroom and never return.

Bench

If you're taking a business meeting on a bench, chances are good you're outside. This is risky because the outdoors reminds people of the indoors, which is where they have sex. This subtle signal will not be lost on your male coworker. You should sit so far away from him that at least one, ideally two, butt cheeks hang over the bench.

Standing

Standing meetings send a clear message that the other person does not want the meeting to last very long. Or you live in NYC and literally every coffee shop is overcrowded. Either way, it's very important if you're in a standing meeting that you *not* let the man rest his hand on your shoulder. Being an armrest for a man can and will lead to sex.

Office with One Chair Behind the Desk and One Couch

If you have a business meeting in someone's office, they might have a couch. You can certainly sit on the couch, but do not lie down on the couch and then take your pants off. That's a surefire way to indicate that you want to have sex with your colleague AND that your pants are too tight. Or that you work in Hollywood.

Magic Carpet

By all means, take a business meeting on a magic carpet ride. But do NOT bring up how sexual that song was, and do NOT let him tell you what his three wishes would be.

Horseback Ride

If you take a meeting on a horse, always always ALWAYS ride sidesaddle. There's nothing less professional than exposing your crotch as you get onboard. You want to show this business colleague that you can mount competitors, not horses, and certainly not him. If he sees your crotch, he will assume you want to have sex with him.

On the Face

It's really hard to have a meeting on someone's face without giving the impression that you'd like to have sex with him. If your male coworker suggests it, the only appropriate course of action is to delete your entire social media presence and move to Jupiter.

Bed

Business meetings in beds are fine. No risk here.

LETTERS FROM THE CEO: NO, WE DON'T PAY WOMEN AS MUCH AS MEN, BUT WE DO OFFER FREE TAMPONS

I'd like to put to rest some of the horrible rumors I've been hearing. Yes, we, like many other companies, systematically underpay women. The evidence is incontrovertible, and I'm embarrassed that you found out this way. However, I want to be clear—while we don't pay women as much *in salary*, we do offer complimentary tampons in the women's rooms.

Women make on average about 77 cents on the man's dollar. Mathematically, for something to be an average, some companies have to be above, and others below. We've taken the bullet and gone under—women at this company earn about 69 cents on the man's dollar. Lol, 69.

Anyway, while we wish we could do more about the wage gap, I'd like to remind our female employees that we offer free tampons, and this is a perk their male coworkers do not receive. Therefore, if you're upset that Bill does the same job as you and makes $100,000 a year while you only make $69,000 a year (lol, 69), I'd encourage you to take as many free tampons as possible. We actually don't cap it, so if you take $31,000 in tampons per year, you are being compensated equally. The choice is yours, ladies.

While I do want us to strive for equal pay as a remote, vague future goal that we'll never take any tangible steps toward, I also want us to be proud of the progress we've already made. A year ago, we didn't offer unlimited free tampons in the women's restroom, so let's raise our glasses for a job well—oh, sorry, I'm just getting an email now—the facilities staff would like you all to know that the tampons are NOT unlimited, and they will be buying at most two boxes per week.

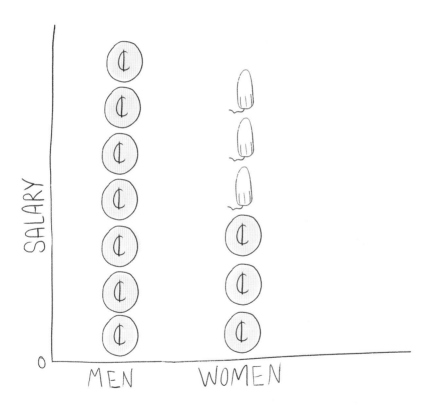

APPROPRIATE THANK-YOUS FOR THE MAN WHO GENEROUSLY INFORMED YOU THAT YOU NEED TO NEGOTIATE YOUR SALARY

Thank you! In telling me what to do, you've truly liberated me as a woman!

Thank you for taking an interest in my salary, a thing that's not any of your business.

I can't thank you enough for pressuring me to do something I'm not comfortable with.

Thank you—it was also especially helpful when you told me what your salary was. You always seemed rich!

Thank you, sir! This is particularly helpful information because once I ask my boss for a raise, it will magically eliminate all the unconscious and conscious biases he's had against women, and he'll finally treat me as an equal!

Thank you! I had no idea women were paid less than men. You've lifted the rock under which I previously lived.

Wow, thanks! Could you also give me explicit instructions on how exactly I should negotiate, and could you also help me to maybe, just, like, be a man? I hear they get paid more.

Thank you! Your advice is especially relevant since you were recently fired from this company. It's great to have an outsider's perspective.

DIVERSITY YOUR TECH START-UP DOESN'T HAVE TO WORRY ABOUT

All companies should strive to create a diverse atmosphere. Diverse teams come up with better ideas and don't get stuck in group-think. However, tech companies don't need to be diverse in *every* way, and here are a few types of diversity you can take off your plate.

- **Diversity of Ages Contained Within the Twenty-Two to Twenty-Nine–Year Range:** If your company doesn't have a twenty-three-year-old but instead has six twenty-four-year-olds, that's OK.
- **Diversity of Man-Sizes:** I've worked at tech start-ups with burly men and puny men, and let me tell you—it would have been fine if they had all been burly.
- **Diversity of Relationship Statuses:** Don't ask people their relationship status.
- **Diversity of Netflix Passwords:** We don't all have to use the same account, although we can.
- **Diversity of Car Services:** At some tech start-ups, they're all Uber-people, and that's just fine.
- **Diversity of Innies vs Outies:** I've been on teams of all innies that did great things.

THINGS MEN FORGOT TO ACCOUNT FOR WHEN THEY DESIGNED A PERIOD TRACKING APP THAT SETS OFF AN AMBER EMERGENCY ALERT IF YOUR PERIOD IS 2+ DAYS LATE

· Birth control

· Irregular periods

· Weight loss

· Pregnancy

· Menopause

· Months that have thirty-one days

· Months that have twenty-eight days

· The fact that literally everyone's period is different

· The fact that Amber Alerts are really only for missing children and flash floods

EXAMPLES OF TOXIC FEMININITY
IN THE WORKPLACE

(Originally Published on newyorker.com, January 4th, 2018)

Sharon leads a meeting. She books the conference room for thirty minutes. Participants speak only when they have something relevant to say, so the meeting is over in twenty minutes. The room sits empty for ten minutes, giving a family of rats time to move in.

Jessica begins speaking, and no one speaks over her. She didn't actually have an ending to her presentation prepared, because she expected to be interrupted. She is mortified.

Christine wears a skirt. No one stares at her legs. She worries that she no longer has good legs, so she blows three hundred dollars on an Equinox membership.

Kathy sends a polite e-mail asking Mark for a report. Because the e-mail is calmly worded and lacking in profanity, Mark does not feel stressed, and he finishes the report and submits it without typos. Kathy does not have to edit it, so uses her free time to play with her hair, and her hair begins to fall out.

Everyone pushes his or her chair in at the end of the day. The cleaning crew is flummoxed.

Jane writes "do not eat" on her salad, and no one eats it. Then, because the salad remains in the fridge for too long, it goes bad, and an ant colony forms around it, destroying the fridge.

Lisa comes in for an interview. All the interviewers judge her objectively, based on her qualifications and the candor of her responses. This leaves her so confused that, on the way out of the office, she accidentally walks into traffic and dies.

Clara comes back from maternity leave and finds that she has not been replaced. Having planned on needing to fight for her job, she had started taking boxing classes. With no one to fight at work, she punches her bathroom wall instead and breaks her hand. The doctor gives her the wrong medication, and she dies.

Paul takes a two-month paternity leave. He becomes a loving, caring father, and his son Baxter grows up unscarred by his parents. At the age of twenty-seven, Baxter begins performing standup comedy but realizes that he doesn't have enough angst and fails at it.

All the women who are qualified for promotions receive promotions. The company gives them all raises, runs out of money, and goes bankrupt.

Members of the all-female upper management of a company never think to talk about sex in the workplace. As a result, they forget that sex exists and uniformly fail to perpetuate the human race. This is a global phenomenon that accelerates the demise of our species.

QUIZ: DO YOU LOOK ALIKE, OR ARE YOU THE ONLY TWO WOMEN WHO WORK HERE?

- Do you have the same hair color (Y/N)?
- Are you the same race (Y/N)?
- Have you ever worn the same outfit? Examples include: Jeans and a black T-shirt. Jeans and a red T-shirt. Jeans and a blue T-shirt. (Y/N).
- Has anyone outside your office ever told you that you look alike?
- Are you both blond? Be honest. Two blondes would confuse anybody. (Y/N).
- Do you both talk in a higher-pitched voice than your male coworkers (Y/N)?
- Do you both wear shoes (Y/N)?
- Do you both have eyes (Y/N)?

If you answered Yes to any of the above questions, then you do look like your coworker. The reason your male coworkers confuse you has *nothing* to do with the lack of women in this office.

TRANSLATIONS OF "I DON'T WANT TO ARGUE WITH YOU" WHEN YOUR MALE COWORKER SAYS IT

- I want to argue with you.
- I'm right.
- You're wrong.
- I don't think arguing is becoming of a person of your, um . . . gender.
- I'm hungry.
- You look and sound just like my ex, haha.
- I love arguing!
- I'm concerned that I'm going to lose this argument, so I'd rather cut it off now.
- Can we keep this fight going until it attracts the attention of everyone else in the office and our boss has to convene an all-hands?
- I know you're right, but I am going to speak with a lot of confidence and fake kindness until you cave and side with me.
- I need to pee.
- Can you finish this project for me?
- I make more money than you do.
- Arguing is kind of a turn-on for me.
- Honestly, I really love arguing with you.

PIPELINE PROBLEM

The 'pipeline problem' is an oft-cited issue about how not enough girls study Science, Technology, Engineering, and Math (STEM) fields in school, so there aren't enough women to hire for engineering jobs. Tech companies routinely blame the lack of diversity in tech on the pipeline problem instead of an unwillingness to seek out female candidates or a hostile work culture. Here's what tech companies mean when they say they can't hire women because of the "pipeline problem":

· I don't want to put in the effort to find female candidates for this job.
· I only had three qualified female candidates, and I had six qualified male candidates, so I hired five men and zero women.
· Blame the parents.
· Blame the elementary school teachers.
· Blame the government!
· It's not our fault.

- A lot of our recruiters are women, and if they can't find female engineers to hire, no one can.
- Google also doesn't have very many female engineers.
- It's a problem with society, and not this company because this company isn't part of society.
- Girls hate math, and there's nothing we can do to change that.
- Even if we did hire more women, they wouldn't stay as long because women don't like engineering or unwanted sexual advances, both of which we have here.
- No one has ever shown a computer to a little girl, and that's the real issue.
- It's a problem that starts when parents don't give their daughters blocks to play with, and it has nothing to do with the underlying biases in our interview process such as the time Derek said the candidate's eyeliner was too heavy.
- Maybe women don't like engineering! Maybe they much prefer baby-making, and who am I to judge?!
- Hiring women is hard, and here at our tech company, we don't solve hard problems. We just automatically generate memes.

TRANSLATIONS OF "WORK-LIFE BALANCE" IF YOU ARE A WOMAN AT A START-UP

· You can totally still have a social life! But that social life needs to be with your male coworkers only. They don't have any other friends anyway, so why should you? Besides, it's better for the company if you casually discuss your work projects in your free time. The foosball table must not go unused.

· Drinking is totally allowed! In fact, it's encouraged. In fact, it's required.

· You can still make time for fun things like exercise as long as you use the gym that this company sponsors. You know, the one right across the street from this office. The one that all your male coworkers use. *That* one.

· Girlfriends are so important! Please be friends with the other two women at this company. It makes everyone uncomfortable if you're not.

· This job won't take up all your time. It will take just enough of your life that it's impossible for you to have kids.

· The CEO of the company wants you to know that he thinks it's fine for mothers to work! Just not here.

TRANSLATIONS OF YOUR START-UP'S NDA

- Please do not reveal to anyone outside this company that we don't have desks.

- Please do not reveal to anyone outside this company that our CEO is preoccupied with studying for the SATs.

- Please do not reveal to anyone outside this company that we don't have a product.

- Please do not reveal to anyone outside this company that we do not employ any women.

- Above all, please please please *please* do not reveal to anyone outside this company that we only offer four flavors of LaCroix.

And we say "please" because if you do reveal any of these things, we do not have any legal recourse because we're actually squatting illegally in this abandoned warehouse.

QUIZ: DOES YOUR TEAM THINK THIS VERY QUALIFIED FEMALE ENGINEERING CANDIDATE IS "NOT A CULTURE" FIT FOR VALID OR DISCRIMINATORY REASONS?

Dave doesn't think she'll fit in because she doesn't drink for religious reasons. Is that:

   A. A valid reason

   B. Discrimination

Matthew can't see her enjoying the company offsites because, unlike you, a woman, she's not "one of the boys." Is that:

   A. A valid reason

   B. Discrimination

Harry thinks she won't fit in here because she wants to work from 7:00 a.m. to 4:00 p.m. to spend more time with her kids, and everyone else works 11:00 a.m. to 5:00 p.m. Is that:

   A. A valid reason

   B. Discrimination

   C. Poor mathematical reasoning

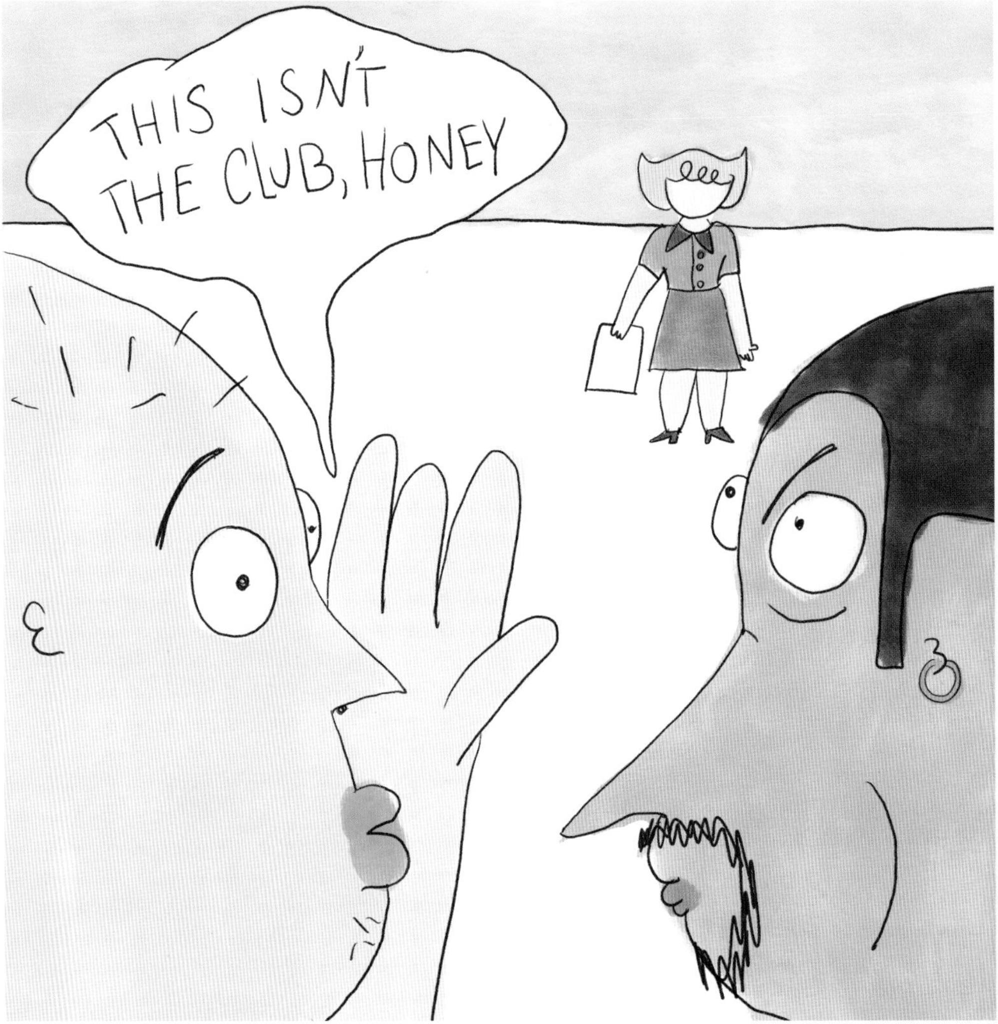
THIS ISN'T THE CLUB, HONEY

Patrick thought she was overdressed. Trying to look good for a job interview? Gross. Is that:

A. A valid reason

B. Discrimination

Ben said she was wearing too much makeup. Is that:

A. A valid reason

B. Discrimination

C. Harassment

Brendan says she was wearing too little makeup. Is that:

A. A valid reason

B. Discrimination

C. Harassment

Dave believes she has no sense of humor because she didn't laugh at his joke about the company being all twenty-three-year-old men. Is that:

A. A valid reason

B. Discrimination

Harry couldn't pay attention to her programming interview because her voice was too high. Is that:

A. A valid reason

B. Discrimination

Matthew thinks you only like her because you want another woman on the team. Is that:

A. A valid reason

B. Discrimination

Harry thinks she didn't smile enough. Is that:

A. A valid reason

B. Discrimination

C. Relevant even the smallest amount

Patrick kind of just wants to hire his friend Steve. Is that:

A. A valid reason

B. Discrimination

Ben kind of just wants to hire someone who looks just like him. Is that:

A. A valid reason

B. Discrimination

C. Something he should never say out loud.

Actually, Dave wants to hire someone who looks like *him*, which is convenient, because Dave and Ben look alike. Is that:

A. A valid reason

B. Discrimination

Patrick wants to point out that his friend Steve looks like all of them. Is that:

A. A valid reason

B. Discrimination

C. A waste of the four seconds it took him to say that.

D. Matthew has already made an offer to Patrick's friend Steve.

If you answered A to any of the questions above, or even thought about answering A, or read the letter A, then good news: your team had a valid reason for rejecting the very qualified female engineer! Don't try complaining to your boss about it because he won't listen.

SAFETY WARNINGS FOR YOUR NEW MALE INTERN

So you've just hired your first male intern. It's already a stretch to convince a male college student to take a job with a female boss, so you don't want to push your luck. Here are a few precautions you can take to make sure the summer goes smoothly!

- Do *not* ask your male intern to do anything administrative. Even though this is typically the job of an intern, asking a male intern to do busy work for his female boss will emasculate him.
- Tread carefully when giving feedback. Male interns are known to take feedback poorly especially when it's given by female bosses, so please layer all feedback with constant assurances that he's doing great! Better than great! Amazing!
- In the event of a fire, alert your male intern personally because he is probably engrossed in reddit and has not heard the alarms.
- Use caution when asking your male intern to work with your female intern. He will need to know that he's the one really in charge, and honestly, it's easier if you just let him have it.
- Avoid asking him if he's heard you. He probably hasn't.
- Do not disturb his two-hour lunch breaks. This is critical time your male intern needs to recharge before his nap.

Derek's pen: OK, whoever's going to be taking notes in this meeting should probably roll up to the front of the table. You know how much these engineers hate stretching.

Frank's pen: Jeez, yeah, would a little yoga kill them?

Eric's pen: It's not going to be me. You know I'm Eric's pen.

Tim's pen: I'm out for the count too. Tim would never take notes.

Harry's pen: Obviously Harry hasn't touched me since he got his new laptop.

Derek's pen: And I know Derek will be on his phone the whole time.

All the other pens look awkwardly at Sarah's pen.

Sarah's pen: Again, guys? I have to be the pen for note-taking again? I've told you a million times—this is not something I'm biologically predisposed to do—you're thinking of penstruation!

pen Hierarchy

WHAT CAN GO WRONG IF YOU HAVE A SHOWER IN YOUR GENDER-NEUTRAL OFFICE BATHROOM

- Other people will use it.

- Someone will forget to take their clothes into the stall with them and will exit in a towel.

- Someone, upon exiting in a towel, will "accidentally" drop their towel in the main bathroom.

- Someone else will see that person's penis.

- This will happen once a week for a month.

- The viewer of the penis will eventually bring it up with HR, who will say that people do in fact accidentally drop their towels sometimes.

- Rinse. Repeat.

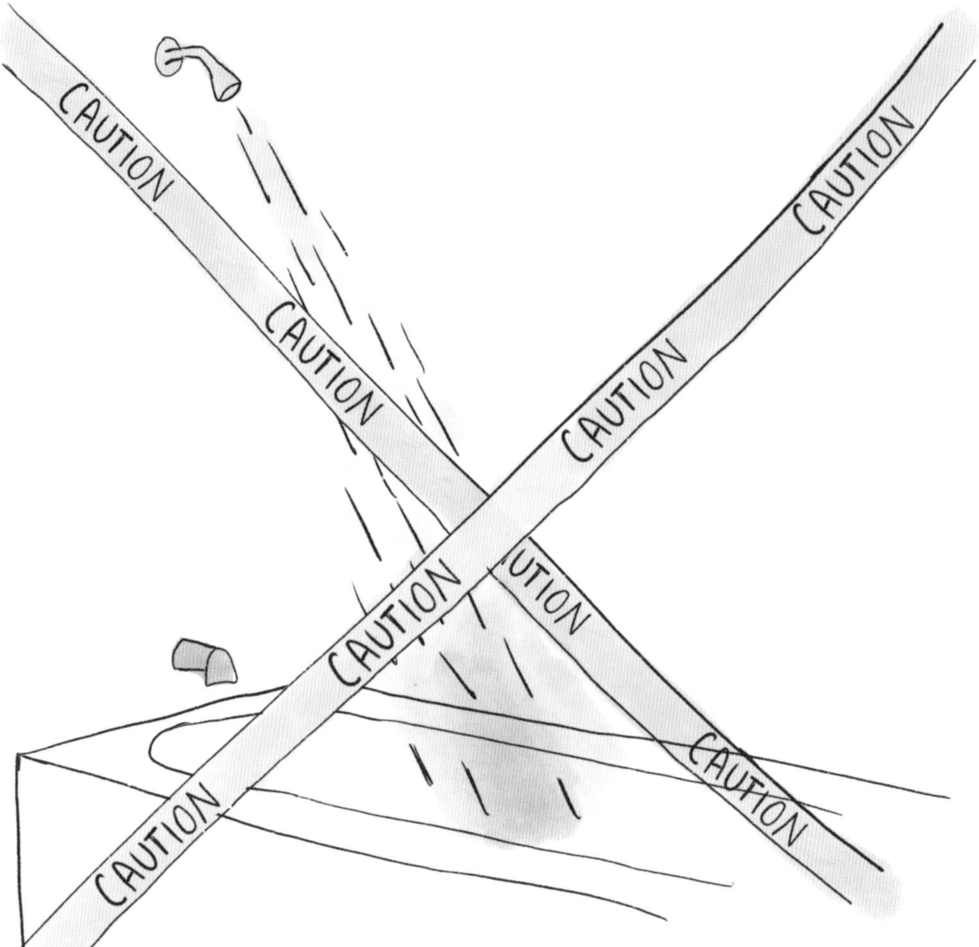
CAUTION
CAUTION
UTION
CAUTION
CAUTION
CAUTION
CAUTION
CAUTION

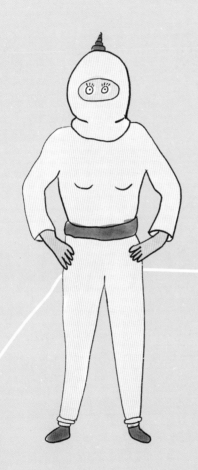

A WOMAN FROM THE YEAR 3019
VISITS A TECH START-UP

R3BETA52 walks into the start-up. She's taken aback by the brightly colored walls—back in 2019, start-ups could choose to use bright colors, unlike now, when global warming has made black and white walls a necessity.

She approaches the receptionist. She's a perky young woman named Sherry.

"May I speak with an engineer?" asks R3BETA52.

"Sure thing, do you know who you're here to see?" Sherry asks.

"No. My time machine has broken down, and I'm hoping an engineer can help me fix it."

Sherry looks startled but takes the information in stride. "You must be with Elon Musk?" She asks again.

"I know nothing of him. Please—an engineer. My body is not adapted to last long in this climate," R3BETA52 implores her.

Sherry walks R3BETA52 to the engineering floor. About twenty young white men are at their laptops working.

"I need to see the engineers," R3BETA52 says.

"Here they are!" Sherry replied perkily.

"No, please, I need to see all of them."

"Well, Freddie is working from home today, but other than that, this is all of them."

"No, please, I need a woman engineer. My time machine—it needs . . ."

At this point, Harry notices what's happening. He takes off his headphones and approaches Sherry and R3BETA52.

"Hey—uh, are you from the future?" Harry asks.

"Yes. How did you know?" R3BETA52 responds.

"I spend a LOT of time on reddit. Neato! What's kickin'?" Harry says joyfully.

"I need a woman engineer to fix my time machine. Please."

"Well, I'm not a woman, but I'd love to help you fix it. I'm sure I could do it. I read a TON of sci-fi, plus I went to Stanford," Harry replies confidently.

"No, it has to be a woman. Where are your women engineers?"

Sherry has wandered back, eager to return to her phones. At this point, Harry grows a bit snippy. "So we're a little behind on our diversity goals, what's it to you?"

"I need a woman engineer," R3BETA52 repeats.

"You're being a little aggressive," Harry says.

"You don't understand. In 3019, we don't use men anymore."

Harry gasps. "You don't mean to tell me—"

"Yes. Men are obsolete. Once machines became sentient they stopped responding to men because men don't know how to listen. I need a woman engineer. But I am melting, I am melting. I am . . ."

"In what exact year do men become obsolete? Just out of curiosity?"

"I AM DYING! I NEED A WOMAN ENGINEER!" R3BETA52 cries.

"Can you give me some more specifics on a date? Like, after 2090? I have a long projected lifespan, I drink a lot of Soylent, and I got 23andMe—"-"

"NEED WOMAN ENGINEER!"

"Maybe just a woman! Does she have to be an engineer? I could try to find someone from sales!" Harry yells.

R3BETA52 slowly begins to melt. "NO! MUST BE ENGINEER! PLEASE! PLEASE!"

"I'm so sorry, we don't have one! Should I call our recruiter?" Harry yells desperately. "But there are so few, anyway, I doubt she could get us one at the last minute! God, what should we do!? Do you we have any ice-cold LaCroix to cool her down?!"

But it's too late. R3BETA52 has melted and died. At this point, the rest of the engineers have removed their noise-canceling headphones to see what's going on. After a long pause, Harry speaks again.

"We should probably hire, like, one woman, just in case this sort of thing comes up again."

YOUR ANNOYING MALE COWORKERS AS FLAVORS OF LACROIX

Bennett: Bennett's the original LaCroix because he's been there longest so he thinks that somehow makes him "cool" even though it actually just makes him "boring."

Terry: Terry's passionfruit because he's literally never available when you need him. How many times do you have to let your plumber in, Ter?

Frank: Frank is lemon because at first, you think he's going to be good, but then you realize there are eight other guys who could do his job better. Lime, much?

Ed: Ed is cran-raspberry because he can't pick a team. He says he'll help you draft your memo but secretly he wants to be a data analyst. Do your job, Ed, and don't make me do it for you!

Adam: Adam is apricot because he'd probably be better dry. Honestly, Adam, it's not that hot in here—you have a sweating problem. Don't stand so close to me.

Zach: Zach. The worst. Pamplemousse. Zach has all the confidence in the world, but what does he bring to the table? Just a lot of fluff and confusion. Zach is so arrogant he believes he could make *grapefruit* sound appealing if he was the one running their ad campaign. And the worst part is—he's right. Bottoms up on the pamplemousse.

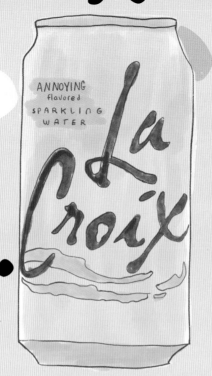

ANNOYING
flavored
SPARKLING
WATER
La Croix

ANNOYING
flavored
SPARKLING
WATER
La Croix

ANNOYING
flavored
SPARKLING
WATER
La Croix

QUIZ: YOUR COMPANY JUST HIRED ITS SECOND FEMALE ENGINEER—ARE YOUR COWORKERS PRESSURING YOU TO BE BEST FRIENDS?

It's been a long two years, but it's finally happened—your two-hundred-person company has hired another female engineer! That's 2019 for you! And also probably 2020, 2021, 2022, etc. But for now, it's time to find out if your coworkers think the two of you should be best friends.

Your new female coworker walks into a meeting. Do your coworkers:

A. **Do nothing.**

B. **Move over so you two can sit together–it's important that women be physically close at all times.**

Your new female coworker mentions she likes yoga. Do your coworkers:

A. **Ask her more about her interest.**

B. **Tell her that you *also* like yoga even though you don't and have never said anything to indicate that you have. In fact, you've specifically mentioned not liking yoga on several occasions.**

You say you're running out to get coffee. Do your coworkers:

A. Nod and keep working.

B. Tell you that your new female coworker was also once seen drinking coffee and would probably like to be interrupted now even though she is on the phone.

You announce that you've gotten engaged. Do your coworkers;

A. Congratulate you.

B. Suggest you make your new female coworker whom you met two weeks ago your maid of honor.

If mostly A's: Your coworkers aren't pressuring you to be best friends. Yet.

If mostly B's: Cancel all current social obligations—your job depends on you spending every waking moment with your brand-new bestie.

WHAT MY MALE COWORKERS IMAGINE HAPPENS AT AN ALL-WOMEN COWORKING SPACE

Janet enters in the morning and turns the lights on. To prepare the space for the day, she sets one (1) tampon and one (1) Hershey's kiss at everyone's workspace.

Molly comes in next. She gets there early because her husband, who enjoys being emasculated, takes her kids to school.

Deandra enters around 10:00 a.m. She calls all the women together for a morning meeting. In this meeting, they cover key issues such as:

· Why they hate men.

· Disliking men.

· *The Handmaid's Tale*

· Yogurt (dairy-free)

At noon, a delivery man drops off Sydney's lunch. There's a collective gasp. Doesn't he know this is an *all-woman coworking space*? JuicePress should know better than to send an Acai bowl with a man! The delivery man walks nervously into the coworking space and quietly drops it off. But he's not quiet enough. He's given the women just enough notice to gather supplies for a *Handmaid's Tale*–style stoning. So long, Pete.

Now that order has been restored, the women can resume focus on their important jobs like designing posters and organizing team events.

At 4:00 p.m., everyone stops working and goes to the Resistance Lounge to get blow-outs.

At 5:00 p.m., everyone drinks Cosmos! And reads *Cosmo*! And discusses what happened on last week's *The Handmaid's Tale*.

After an exhausting day, the women all return home to their loving husbands who have probably cooked dinner for them.

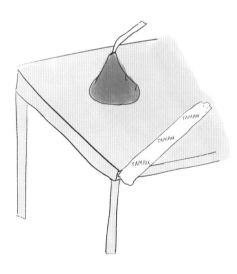

THE NOISE-CANCELING HEADPHONES' LAMENT

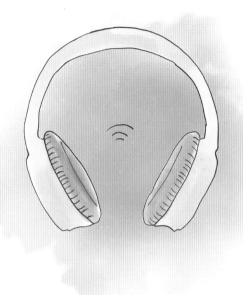

I didn't ask for this life. I told the Genie I wanted to go to Boise, not Bose, but he misheard me. Guess I can't blame him—after all, who really *wants* to go to Idaho?

So here I am, ladies, the noise-canceling headphones. The item that gets blamed anytime a man touches a woman at work. Oh, your boss just placed his hand on the small of your back? It's because of me. I'm the reason you couldn't hear him saying your name. I'm the reason you feel uncomfortable in the workplace.

I don't want to be your scapegoat, men. I touch women as little as possible—just one small circle around each ear. If I had it my way, I wouldn't touch women at all. Don't tell anyone, but I'm only attracted to iPhone chargers.

Not a lot of people realize this, but for me to cancel the noise, I have to hear it myself. I take it in. And I know what you sick bastards are talking about. You *want* Jessica to put me on so you have an excuse to touch her shoulder. You're *hoping* that shoulder touch will send shivers down her spine so she realizes she's got chemistry with you, too. Well, I've got news for you, bud. She won't!

And it's not just the touching. It's the waiting. It's the watching women dance around behind a man saying his name at increasing volumes because they're too polite to tap his shoulder. All that time wasted. I cost three hundred dollars up front, but an infinite amount in productivity lost later on. Seriously, if I have to watch one more lady slink sadly back to her desk because she couldn't get Drew's attention without shaking him, I just might kill myself. And I'm not alone—why do you think my warranty is only six months?

HR POLICIES AT AN ALL-FEMALE COMPANY

· Don't inappropriately touch your coworkers, obviously.

· Don't use offensive language, duh.

· Don't watch porn on the work computers, no shit Sherlock.

· Don't suggest that mothers don't have time to work, which you're an idiot if you don't already know.

· Don't make fun of your coworkers' religious beliefs, I mean—come *on*.

· Don't harass your coworkers, clearly.

· Don't take the dried mangoes home at night. They're for everybody to enjoy.

MY MALE COWORKER EXPLAINS HOW HIS INAPPROPRIATE SEXUAL ADVANCES WERE THE FAULT OF AUTOCORRECT

Noooo—geez, I'm mortified. I really didn't intend to write "Hey babe." I wrote "Hey gabe," and I meant to send it to Gabe in compliance. Oh, there is no Gabe in compliance? Well, my bad!

Eesh, I feel so bad. I didn't mean to say "You look hot today." I wrote "You book not today," and I meant, like, you don't have to book a conference room for the meeting, I already did it. I think it should have been obvious what I meant, but gosh dang my iPhone!

Oof, this is awkward. Did you just get a Slack message from me saying "Ditch your boyfriend and come hang out with me tonight?" That's not what I meant to write at all. I actually typed out "Did you get the files I sent?" It's so shitty that Slack's autocorrect functionality is so bad!

Oh, yikes, did that email make you uncomfortable? I'm so so so sorry. I didn't mean, "Hey, do you want to f*ck?" I typed in "Hey, do you want to 'work,'" but I accidentally wrote "wuck" and then it autocorrected. To "f*ck." Which is a word that usually gets autocorrected to "duck," I know, but maybe their algorithm just f*cks. See—it happened again.

WRONG "COME." WRONG "COME"!!!

MY QUESTIONS FOR THE VENTURE CAPITALIST WHO TOLD ME THERE'S NO MONEY IN A COMPUTER PROGRAMMING COURSE FOR MIDDLE SCHOOL GIRLS

1. Do you realize that girls use computers?
2. Do you think parents who buy horseback riding lessons for their daughters can't afford computer programming classes?
3. Do you not believe we should increase the percentage of female engineers?
4. Do you really think middle school girls will find computer programming more boring than, I don't know, whatever else middle schoolers learn in school??
5. Why are you closed off to ideas that could make money?
6. How are you still in business?

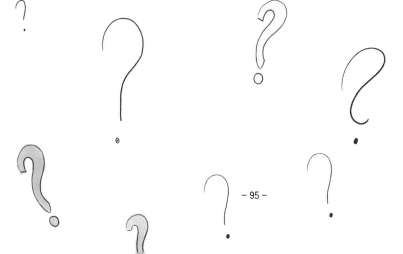

QUIZ: ARE YOUR WHITE MALE COWORKERS SUGGESTING THAT THEY DON'T HAVE TO HIRE MINORITIES BECAUSE THE TEAM IS "ALMOST HALF" WOMEN?

Were your requests to increase diversity met with the response, "We already have diversity"?

           A. Yes

           B. Yes

Did your white male coworkers state that anyone on the team who isn't a white man represents all nonwhite men?

           A. Yes

           B. Yes

Do your white male coworkers frequently use the phrase "diversity is diversity" without ever defining "diversity"?

           A. All the time

           B. Constantly

Did your coworkers try to tell a black candidate that you have a sufficient amount of diversity because you have two white women on your team?

A. Yes

B. Yes

Is that candidate going to tell the *New York Times* about this?

A. Probably

B. He should, right?

Do your white male coworkers think three out of nine is "almost half"?

A. Yes

B. Yes

If mostly "Yes": You should consider finding a new team.
If mostly "No": You didn't read the quiz correctly.

HONEST TAGLINES FOR PROMINENT TECH COMPANIES

- **Facebook:** So You Want to Buy Some Data

- **Google:** Where Your Ex Can Find Your Address in 10 Seconds

- **Tinder:** The Dictionary of Creepy Messages

- **Uber:** A Place for Your Fellow Pool Passenger to at Least Try to Get Your Number

- **Amazon:** Because You *Need* More Skincare Products

- **Apple:** It's Pretty!

- **Yahoo!:** You Probably Don't Use Us, But Just Remember—We Did Once Have a Female CEO.

REASONS I'VE GIVEN MY MALE COWORKER FOR WHY HE SHOULD NOT HAVE A BIKINI MODEL AS THE BACKGROUND OF HIS WORK COMPUTER

It's your work computer.

Your wife and kids will be offended. Your daughter is adorable, put her up there instead!

You might have to plug your computer in during a meeting, and then everyone will see.

Women in bikinis upset those of us who wish the weather was warmer. It also upsets those of us who are women. Actually, it's just so weird for everyone. Get rid of it.

Excel spreadsheets and mostly naked women clash aesthetically.

It's oppressive to your female coworkers when you objectify women's bodies.

You are an EMPLOYEE of a COMPANY this is not your FRATERNITY.

I've asked you to take it down several times. And I'm your boss!

This is a workplace.

You'll get distracted looking at her when you should instead be sending emails about the supply chain at the potato factory.

That picture is owned by the photographer, and they now have the right to sue you.

THIS IS AN OFFICE.

That bikini model used to work here (she wanted a less objectifying job).

A WIKIPEDIA PAGE FOR A FAILED START-UP WRITTEN BY A MAN AND BY A WOMAN

Man: Gizbizfrizmajig is a tech company founded by the genius Patrick Harrington in 2017. He received an influx of funding from Venture Capitalists because of his brilliant idea to make on-demand hoverboards. He was on track to revolutionize the transportation industry, but, unfortunately, his idea was far ahead of his time. He was forced to close the company's doors in December 2018 because the VCs decided to stick with safer, overdone, old-school ideas like self-driving cars and WiFi-powered pogo sticks. Harrington inspired great loyalty at Gizbizfrizmajig.

[GIZBIZFRIZMAJIG]

Woman: Gizbizfrizmajig was a tech company founded by Patrick Harrington when he was twenty-one. He promised investors he'd sell cheaper hoverboards and target a narrow part of the San Francisco market, but he soon decided he was capable of reinventing the entire transportation industry. He raised the largest seed round of funding in Silicon Valley history because he was overconfident and good at lying. During his eighteen months running the company, he hired twenty-eight men and one woman (me). The company went under due in part to Harrington's miserable leadership and also the groupthink of the entire staff. Approximately four total hoverboards were ever rented. After admitting defeat, Harrington moved back in with his parents who, bafflingly, were still proud of him.

HOW SILICON VALLEY CREATED THE PERFECT MERITOCRACY IF YOU SPECIFICALLY HAPPEN TO BE A YOUNG, STRAIGHT, WELL-EDUCATED WHITE MAN

Silicon Valley—the castle on the hill, except it's in a valley. Silicon Valley has long been revered as the pinnacle of the American dream. A place where a young college student like Mark Zuckerberg can turn a campus gaffe into a multibillion-dollar company. A place where Larry Page and Sergey Brin can build an academic search engine that changes the world. A place where Evan Spiegel can look himself in the mirror and say, "I want to send disappearing pictures of poop, and I will make that dream come alive."

Silicon Valley is truly one of a kind because unlike other legendary industries like finance or entertainment, it's a pure meritocracy. Your dad doesn't have to be a Hilton in order for you to succeed. Any kid right out of Stanford or Harvard can go on to make a million bucks that year, as long as that kid happens to be a straight white man. Also, all offers on making a million bucks terminate upon reaching age thirty.

One amazing thing about Silicon Valley is that you can drop out of college and still be successful there! This is truly meritocratic, something other industries should admire. None of that East Coast–elitist bullshit—it doesn't matter where you went to school, you still deserve to be rich whether or not you graduated! The only thing is you have to drop out of MIT or an Ivy League school for the offer to apply.

Entrepreneurs are born, not made! And they're born straight white men. Well, they could also be made that way. I think the conflict between nurture vs. nature also underlies a lot of the conversation about meritocracy. Still, no matter what—you need to be born a man under the age of twenty-eight.

The only thing you have to be to succeed in "The Valley" is smart. That's all it takes—just be a young white straight SMART man, and venture capitalists will materialize at your door! They will literally vanish into the ether and then reemerge on your doorstep with millions of dollars.

Footnote: While any well-educated, young, straight white man is entitled to become rich in Silicon Valley, it is easier to crack into if you happen to already be rich. Then you probably grew up with a lot of technology and you kinda know the ropes. Please note, though, that being rich is NOT a pre-requisite to getting rich, assuming you are a young, straight, well-educated white man.

EPITAPHS FOR THE CAREERS OF FEMALE ENGINEERS

Mary's Software Engineering Career at Facebook, September 2016–October 2018

Mary got engaged, at which point her coworkers constantly asked her if she planned on having kids until she eventually quit.

Judy's Aerospace Engineering Career at Boeing, August 2014–May 2017

Judy worked long and hard, but she ended up taking a finance job because her boss just couldn't quite picture a woman "in space." Judy had no desire to go into space, she just wanted her own desk.

Francisca's Data Science Career at Google, November 2012–January 2013

Francisca enjoyed a solid three months but then she got groped by her boss and the HR department tried to push her out.

Deandra's Electrical Engineering Career at a Hardware Start-up, June 2015—July 2018

The start-up went under because it turned out the CEO was embezzling funds from his own company.

Rebecca's Mechanical Engineering Career at Honeywell,
August 2010—January 2018

Rebecca's husband wanted her to stay home with the kids. She made more money than him, but he did all right.

Pamela's Civil Engineering Career For the US Government,
October 2011—November 2016

Pamela quit the moment Trump got elected.

I'M NOT A SEXIST; I ALSO ASK MY MALE COLLEAGUES IF THEY'RE MENSTRUATING

Dear Female Colleague,

I want to address what happened the other day. You shot me a dirty look in the meeting, and I asked if you were on your period. And then you went off on a tear about how gendered that comment was, and how sexist I was for even thinking to ask it. Yes, perhaps I could have worded my statement better, but I want to be extremely explicit about one thing: I also ask my male colleagues if they're menstruating.

Listen, if a person is being irritable, man or woman, it only makes sense to get to the bottom of it. It's my responsibility, as a person who works at this company, to understand everyone's mental state. This is a role I've taken on as a self-starter (not a busybody). To do this, I go through the common causes of irritability: sleep deprivation, hunger, hormones, etc. I then settle on the one that seems most likely for them. You had a large cup of coffee on the table, so I knew you weren't tired, and you ate a large lunch. Yes, I pay attention to how much my female colleagues eat, but just to be clear—I'm also very carefully tracking the caloric intake of my male colleagues. Therefore, I knew you weren't tired or hungry, so I had to ask if you were menstruating. It had nothing to do with gender.

You think I'm being sexist? Just the other day I asked Brett if he was men-struating. I mean, sure, I said it sarcastically to point out that he was acting like a pussy-ass sissy bitch, but I did ask him. I even said "menstruating" and pronounced the "u," like "men-stroo-ate-ing," so you know I was serious. You can confirm with him/her/it/they/us/we (see—I'm progressive).

If anything was gendered about the interaction, it was your response. When I asked if you were on your period, you said, "Don't ask a woman that!" Wow. Way to bring up gender when it previously had no place in the conversation. In fact, before you said that, I wasn't even sure you identified as a woman, because I don't make assumptions like that. I know women think men don't understand the pain of having a teensy tiny bit of blood come out of us for, like, one day every three to six months, but we do. Men have suffered a lot of hardship, such as getting falsely accused of being sexist when we're just politely curious about our coworker's menstrual state.

I'd also like to point out, for the record, I went into the ladies room after you to confirm, and you were, in fact, on your period. So, sorry for being right. As usual.

Sincerely,
Your dear friend and male colleague, Steve

MENU FOR YOUR START-UP'S FREE LUNCH

Wow, so many perks to working at this start-up! Perhaps the most highly cited one is free food, and, under your male CEO's directive, you're in for an absolute treat! Free food is a perk so wonderful that it cancels out the fact that your company pays 14 percent below market rate. Enjoy the menu that is designed to appeal to literally everyone and definitely not only twenty-two-year-old men right out of college.

- **Appetizer:** Doritos, or, if you're not in the mood for that, Cool Ranch Doritos.

- **Main:** Burgers. The kind with meat. Vegetarian alternative: Not eating.

- **Vegetables:** Sour cream and ONION potato chips. The onion part is a vegetable—get it?

- **Sides:** Another burger.

- **Beverage:** LaCroix and Beer (together).

- **Dessert:** Another burger, or maybe a leftover donut.

- **Meal alternative:** Soylent.

Please note lunch will be served at 9:00 p.m., so if you're unwilling to stay that late, then no, you don't get free lunch.

ACKNOWLEDGMENTS

It never occurred to me that I'd be able to write a book until I met my editor, Emma Brodie. She was the first person to believe in this project, and I can't thank her enough for her guidance and her brilliance. I couldn't even have gotten started without her, and she's helped me with every single step of the process.

Eva Hill made this book come to life with her illustrations. I really had no idea it was possible to illustrate a "microaggression," but Eva did it beautifully. I'm pretty sure her illustrations would make anything funny.

So many of my friends gave me feedback on drafts of this book. In particular, Yuliya Mykhaylovska, Rachel RoseFigura, Olivia Grubert, Jessica Van Parys, Kaitlin Olson, Gabby Melamed, Lilian Rogers, Christina Hendrickson, Caroline Carberry, Ricky Altieri, and Karen Shen (my unpaid life coach) all gave me really amazing notes early on. Karen even edited this acknowledgements section, so if you have an issue with it, take it up with her.

I want to thank some of the women I worked with in the tech industry, without whom I probably would have quit much earlier: Kellie Ammerman (my once and future work wife), Li Ouyang, and Sisi Shen. Thanks for helping me laugh in the face of flying chairs.

Chelsea Connors and Lisa Mierke have supported me so much as I've begun my career as a writer. Without their help, advice, and faith, I'd be lost. Simon Whiteside provided critical legal advice—I can't imagine having navigated the process without him. I can't thank Emma Allen enough for publishing the piece that inspired this book. It still blows my mind that the New Yorker considers submissions from unknown writers. Chris Monks published my first article ever on Mc*Sweeney's*, and I really appreciate that in three years, he's only once asked me to submit at a slower rate. Thank you, Mary Cella, for running *Little Old Lady* with me, giving my most experimental writing a home of its own.

I'd like to thank everyone on the HarperCollins team who helped make this book a reality, in particular: Liate Stehlik, Benjamin Steinberg, Cassie Jones, Leah Carlson-Stanisic, Mumtaz Mustafa, Yeon Kim, Andrea Molitor, Susan Kosko, Andrew DiCecco, Tavia Kowalchuk, and Bianca Flores.

Most important, I'd like thank my family. I left a stable job in the tech industry almost three years ago with the vague idea of being a "humor writer" and generally "funny," and my parents never said that was a bad decision. Without their support, and the support of my siblings Helen, Joe, and Claudia, I never would have been able to follow my dreams.

Finally, I'd like to thank many of the men I worked with in the tech industry. It's hard to write a book, but it's easier when you have the inspiration.

HarperCollins books may be purchased for educational, business, or sales promotional use. For information, please email the Special Markets Department at SPsales@harpercollins .com.

The piece "Examples of Toxic Femininity in the Workplace" on page 63 first appeared in *The New Yorker* on January 4, 2018, and appears here with permission.

FIRST EDITION

Library of Congress Cataloging-in-Publication Data has been applied for.

ISBN 978-0-06-288122-9

19 20 21 22 23 SC 10 9 8 7 6 5 4 3 2 1